CULTURAL DJ

Multiplying Creativity by Remixing the World

BY NORMAN MAYERS + SUSANNE HEITZ

IN MEMORY OF

DJ CHEESE + MC MOMA

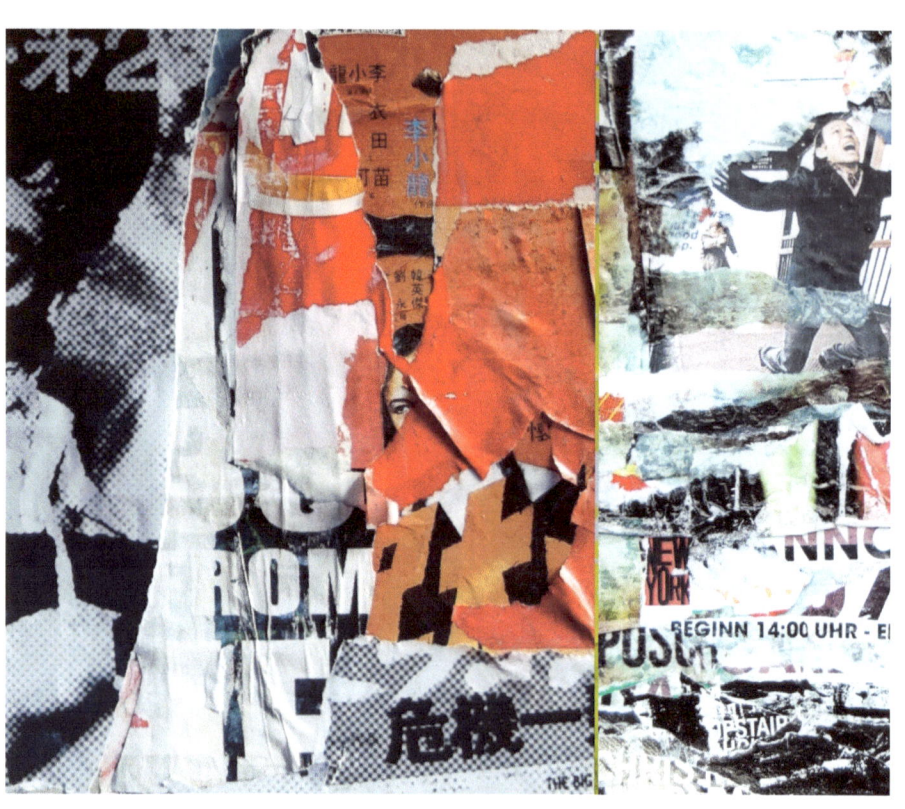

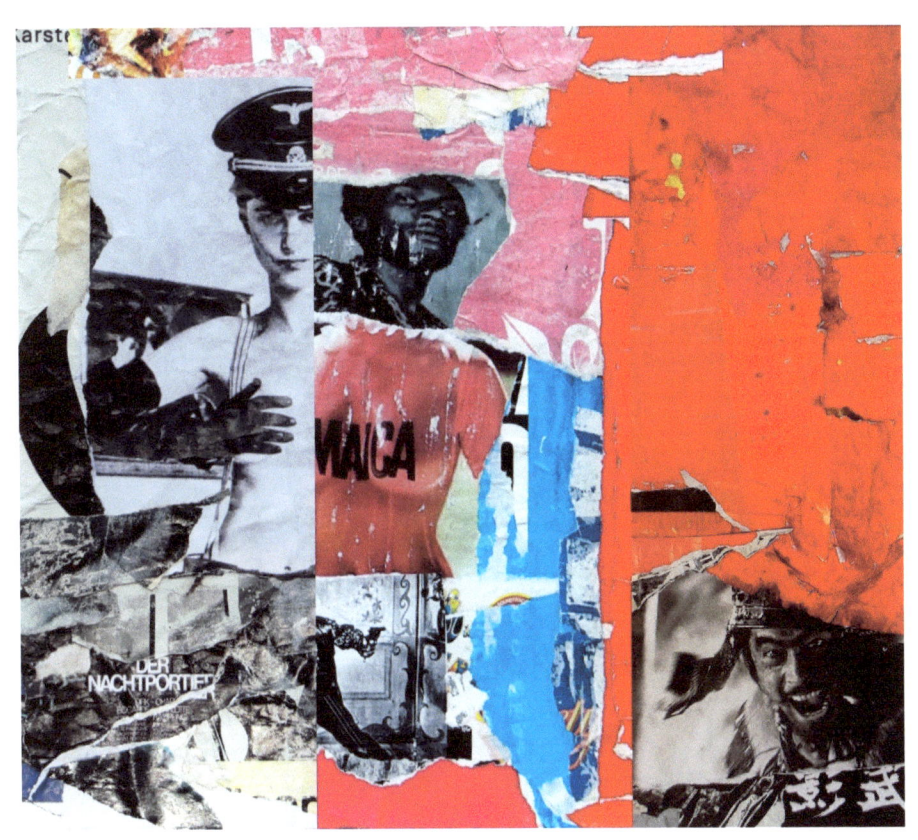

EVERYTHING IS A REMIX WHEN STRANGERS MEET

— Kirby Ferguson Yo Yo Ma

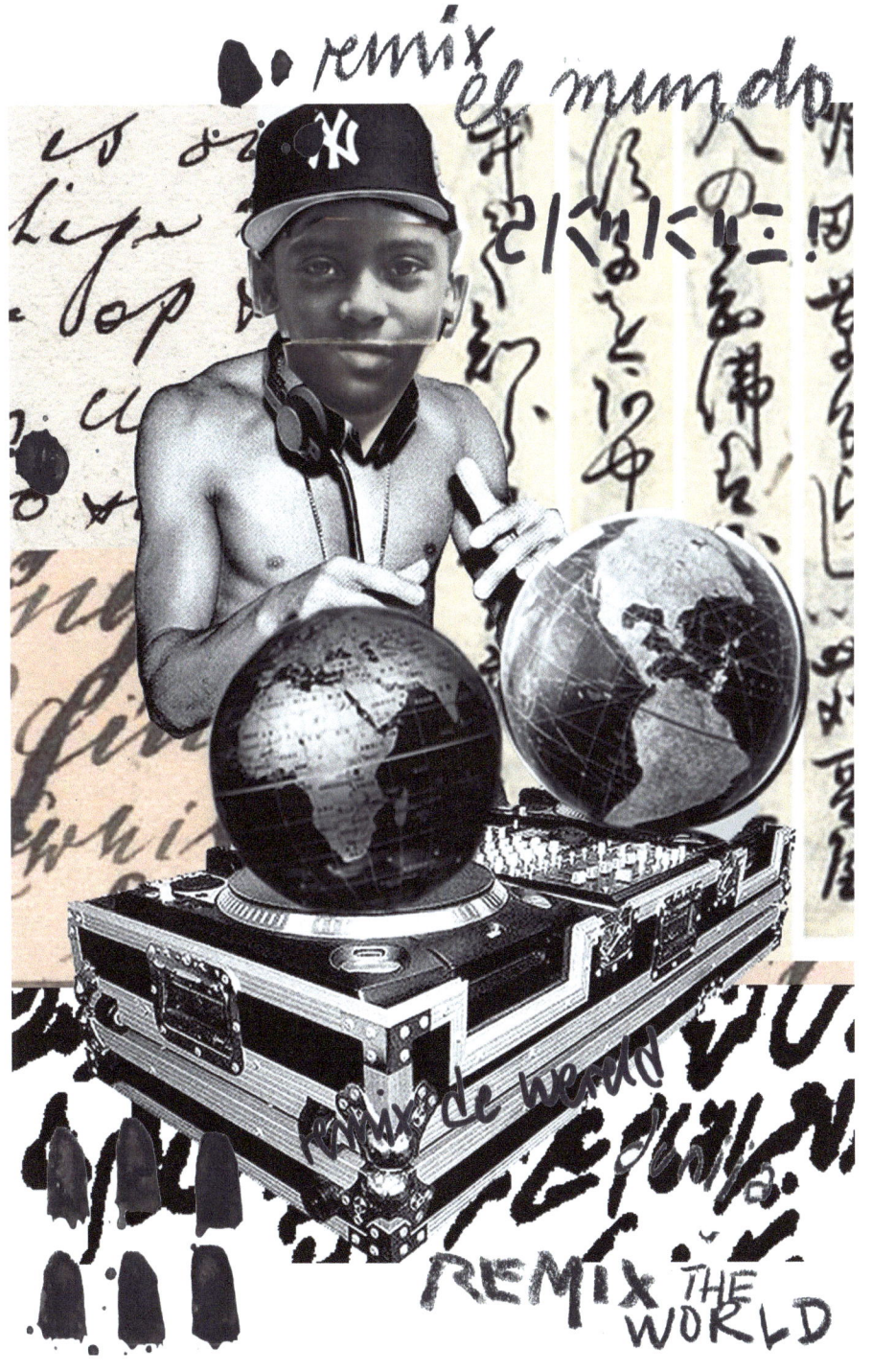

INTRODUCTION

We believe that the world is currently experiencing a fundamental shift in how we create - which is causing our national borders to be superseded by our connectivity. A new generation of creative nomads from across the globe is discovering that the more collaborative we are, the more creative we become.

The motivation to write CULTURAL DJ has its roots in us recognizing the power of this rapidly growing movement. A global movement driven by open-minded, passionate creators who understand the amazing tool of creative cultural collaboration. CULTURAL DJ stands for the groundbreaking approach based on the idea of bringing together diverse creative allies, their unique ideas, thoughts and philosophies.

Our aim is to foster these new cross-cultural links by providing both experienced creative professionals and young creators with the knowledge of how to connect and collaborate across borders. We truly believe that cultural empathy should be the cornerstone of the creative process.

One of the first steps to become a Cultural DJ is to simply enhance your cultural I.Q. and challenge 'traditional' boundaries through creativity. Stepping out of your cultural comfort zone will become an exciting exercise that paves the way to understanding how other cultures perceive our world.

CULTURAL DJ aims to excite you about how becoming a Cultural DJ can unleash the limitless power of creators from any place in the world to turn perceptions inside out, to connect, to collaborate - and induce a creative revolution.

- NORMANSUSANNE

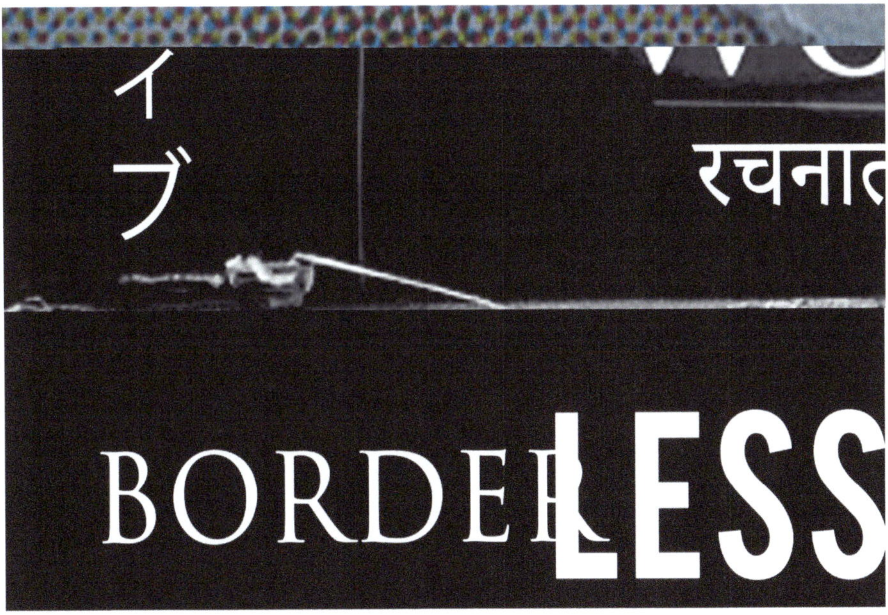

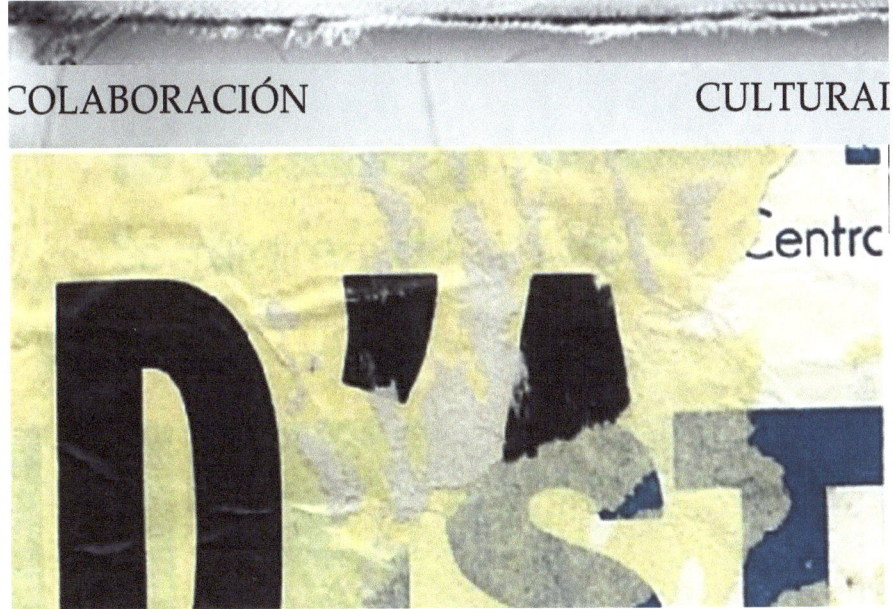

The story of the Cultural DJ begins with the birth of an underground urban movement, known today as hip-hop. This was a transformative moment in world history, because it was the time when a group of multicultural teenagers in the Bronx, NYC, invented something that would have a massive impact on the global creative landscape. These young creators started mixing, combining and fusing elements from their culture with the world and prompted a creative revolution that introduced us to a new form of expression filled with endless possibilities: the REMIX.

By sampling music from across the globe, the early DJs crossed social barriers and drew on elements from multiple cultures. They embraced cultural diversity and began to...

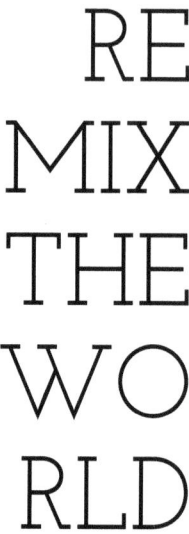

RE
MIX
THE
WO
RLD

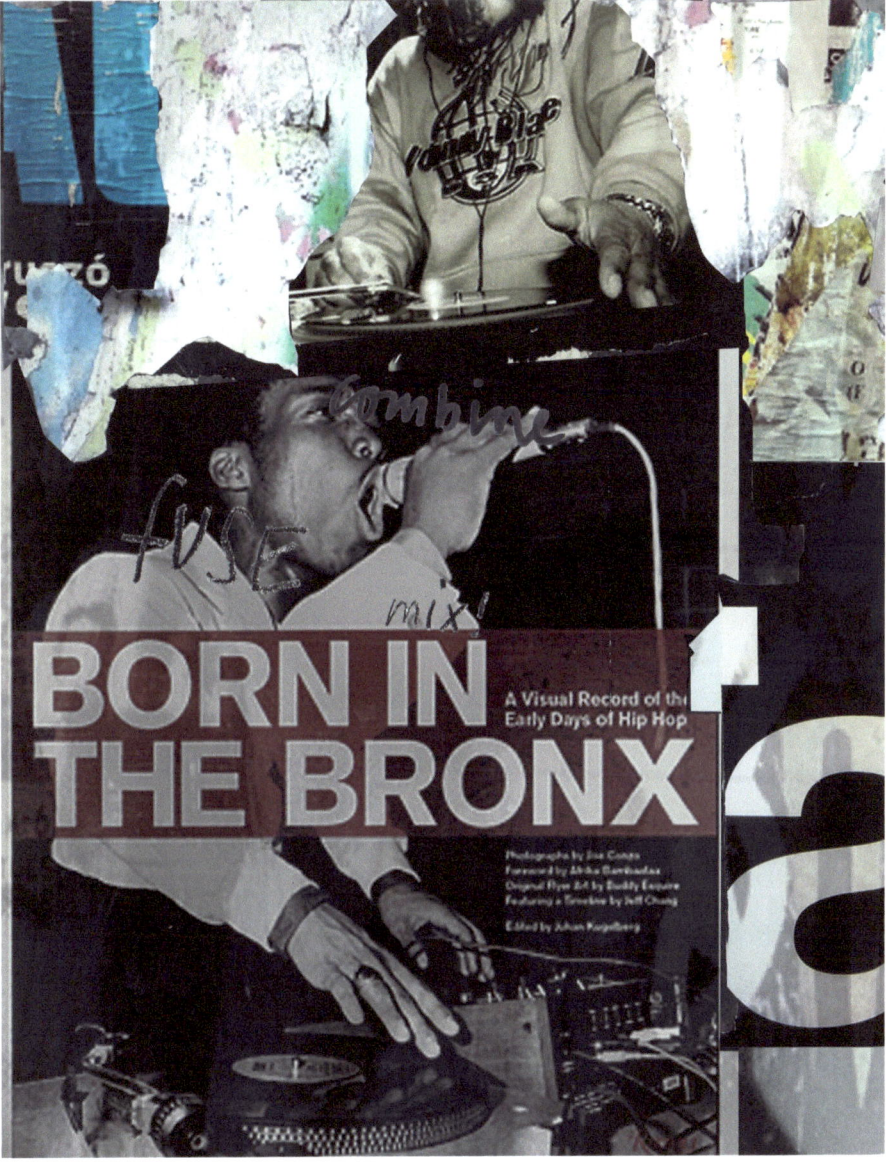

We believe that all creativity, all ideas come from the (re)mixing of existing ideas. At its core, cultural DJing is simply about what happens when different cultural experiences are mixed, combined, and then fused.

Cultural DJs from around the world have the power to cut across borders, languages, generations, genres and cultures to help develop the art of thinking uniquely - together. By leveraging the benefits of the world's diversity and developing creative cultural collaborations from anywhere in the world, creators will deliver innovation.

When we started to envision the concept of remixing the world, we considered what's driving it and why it's happening now. Presently there is a growing borderless creative community discovering that the best results are achieved through collaboration. Fostering the relationship between creativity and cultural diversity develops innovative cultural hybrids. Our creativity is excelling by inviting the strange, the unknown, the unthinkable. And never before has it been more important or easy to be connected to the world.

There are two main factors involved in answering the question: "Why now?"

The FIRST, obviously, is technology. The Internet is causing us to rethink our national geographic borders - crossing them has become as simple as going online. In the borderless world of the Internet, the merging of two or more cultures is inevitable. People who navigate through culturally diverse social media networks can engage automatically in cross-cultural exchanges all day long.

The SECOND factor includes increasing migration into cities and an expanding generation of people with mixed heritage. These demographic changes naturally mean a cumulative level of diversity that creates more opportunities for cross-cultural exchanges.

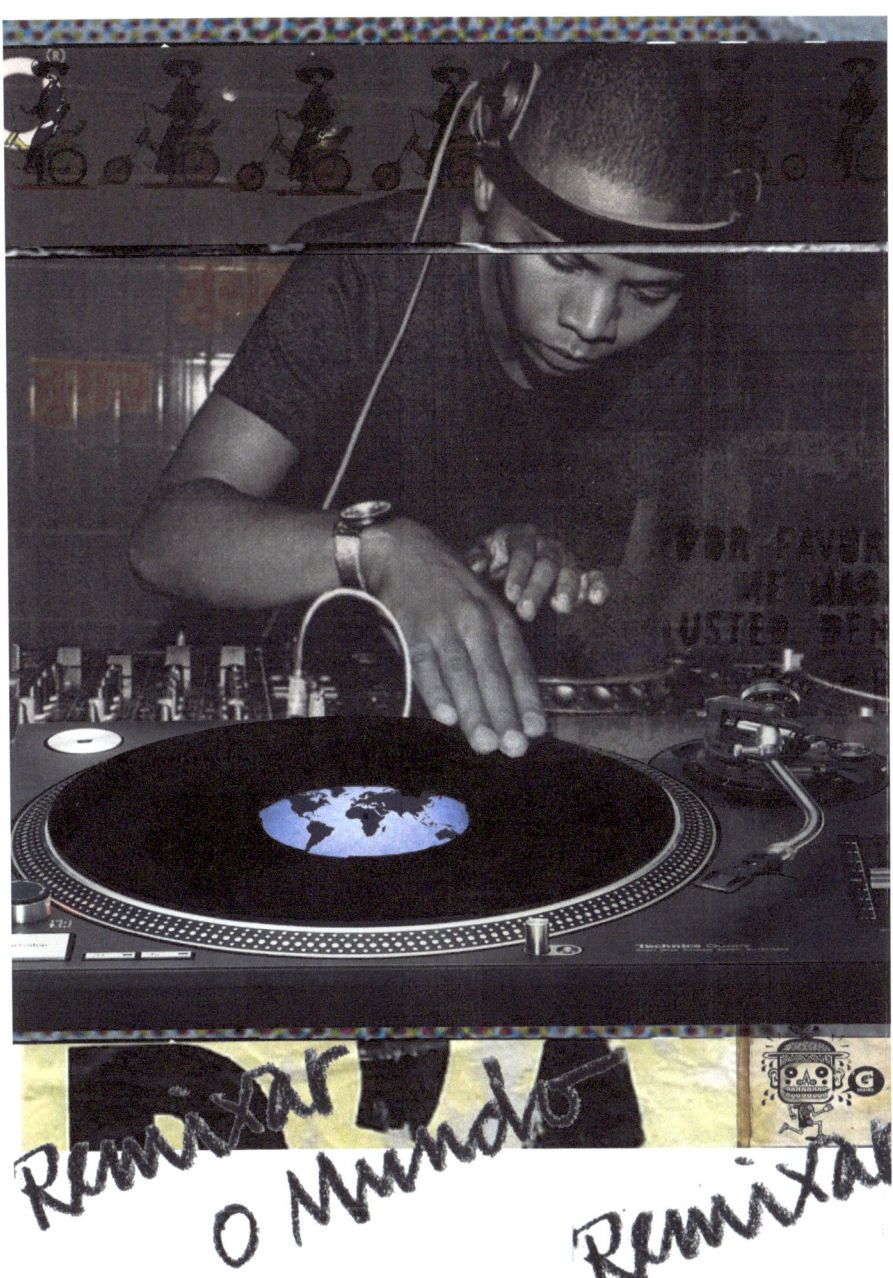

We are now more connected to ever increasing numbers of people who are different from us

than ever before.

In fact, we have become a global creative tribe full of world citizens with diverse backgrounds and experiences. Understanding how to collaborate with people from different cultures is a necessary or even required skill for any person working in a creative field such as art, music, dance, film, advertising, digital technology, publishing, the performing arts, architecture, photography or design.

The extent to which a city's growing cultural diversity is a strong source of creativity, innovation and - ultimately - a competitive advantage has been documented in recent studies conducted by the Center for Urban Research in New York and Stanford University, among others. In his book 'The Rise of the Creative Class' Richard Florida remarks that the level of diversity and creativity is the basic indicator of innovation in cities all around the world.

MIX COMBINE FUSE

Decades of research by organizational scientists, psychologists, sociologists, economists and demographers have resulted in significant proof of the fact that socially and culturally diverse groups are more innovative than homogeneous groups - and this is happening not only because people with different backgrounds contribute novel information. Additionally, by interacting with individuals who are different, creators are encouraged to anticipate alternative viewpoints to re-imagine, to be prepared for collaboration, and to expect that reaching a consensus will take effort.

History teaches us that important breakthrough cultural innovations happen when creative people from diverse cultures come together. This holds true in our current global landscape - innovation will always thrive at the intersection of cultural diversity + creativity.

The world today exposes us to an ever growing source of diverse opportunities. More and more people integrate and blend together, and our daily interactions become multicultural learning experiences. Importantly, the friction that often occurs when diverse cultures clash may present the opportunity to break barriers nurturing innovation through cross-pollination.

As it becomes more multi-ethnic than ever before, our world boasts an emerging global generation of people with mixed heritage for whom multicultural exchanges has become unavoidable. We have now arrived at a point where it is getting exceedingly difficult to detect individual cultural identities. The fact is that the majority of people are an amalgam of cultures. We have all become minorities.

Personal identity is gaining weight over national identity, which causes shifts in how individuals perceive their sense of belonging. These multi-local, global citizens combine in themselves an entire fusion of diverse cultures and re-interpret their own mix again and again through their very own personal filters, defining their style, way of communication, mannerism etc. - and this way play a key role in the creation of ever changing cultures.

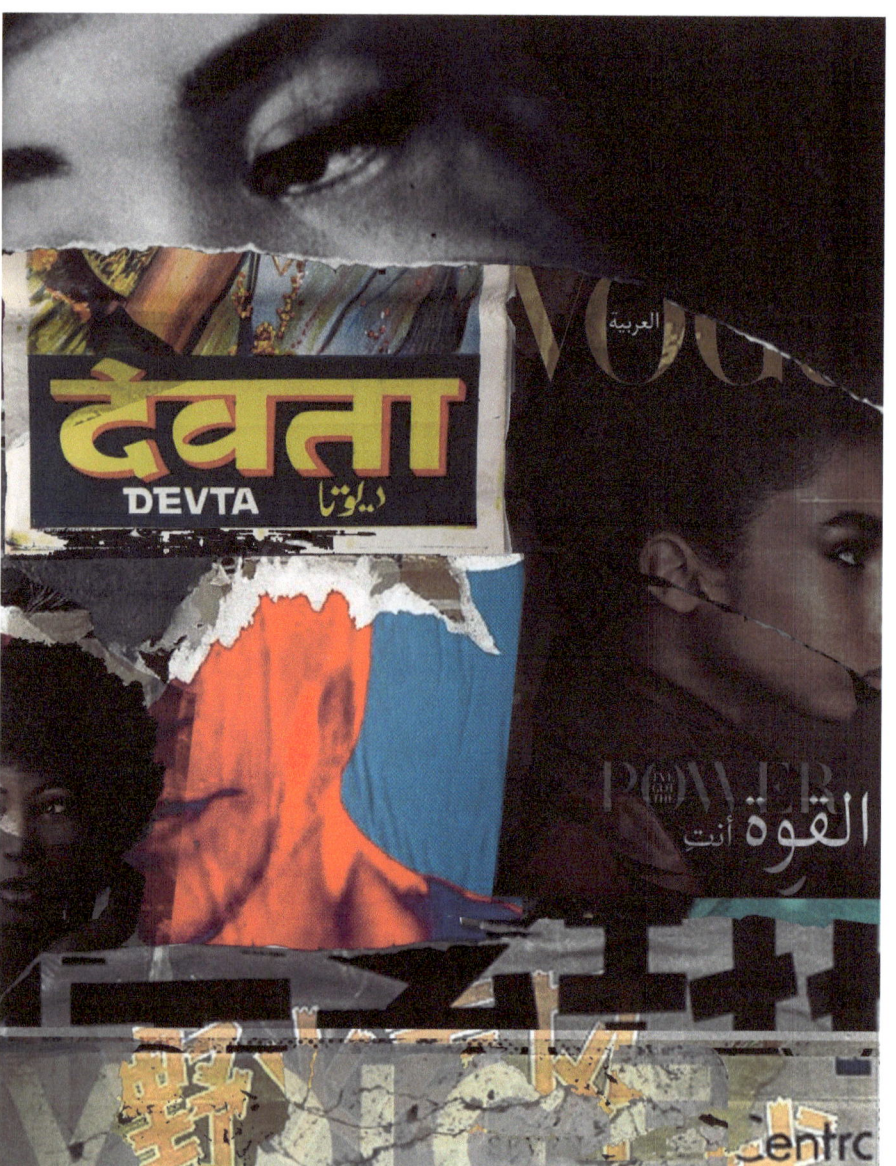

EMBRACE THE STRANGE

Embracing the strange is a mainstay of cultural DJing. Being a Cultural DJ means leaving the familiar behind and becoming a stranger in a foreign land - abandoning the preconceived ideas that limit one's openness to the new. The transformation of perceptions emerges as an antidote for the stale and the traditional.

Cultural DJs roam around in the dark and discover new connections or cause new collisions. For creators, this is an excellent way to prompt doing something they have never done before.

If we don't get lost, we'll never find

a new route.

-Joan Littlewood

LETTING THE WORLD INSPIRE YOU

TRADITIONAL WAYS OF GETTING INSPIRED

WATCH A MOVIE	FIND AN INTERNATIONAL FILM FESTIVAL
VISIT A MUSEUM	GO TO ART GALLERIES THAT SHOWCASE DIFFERENT CULTURES
READ A BOOK	LOOK THROUGH A MAGAZINE IN ANOTHER LANGUAGE
TAKE A WALK	STROLL AROUND IN A CULTURALLY DIVERSE PART OF TOWN
SURF THE NET	JUMP ON A PLANE!

GETTING INSPIRED

'Traditional' methods of getting inspired can be, for example, be surfing the net, watching a movie, visiting a museum, reading a book, taking a walk, etc. But the goal of Cultural DJs is not just getting inspired but letting the world inspire them. If you want to spark your inspiration using the borderless approach, try to jump on a bus, train, or plane instead of surfing the net. Or look slowly at some unknown films at an international film festival instead of just watching a Hollywood blockbuster, and re-frame the familiar by visiting a museum that showcases work from an international artist, or look at a magazine in a different language than your own to see what others overlook. Change your perspective!

One of our favorite ways to do this is to just take a day-trip strolling around an ethnically diverse and unfamiliar part of town and interacting with people who live there.

Letting the world inspire you is like walking through a doorway that leads to endless new relationships and unexpected solutions. Which requires one main trait:

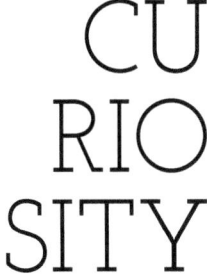

CU
RIO
SITY

Curiosity for us is one of the most important ingredients in the creative process. When you become a Cultural DJ, your personal creative process will always be driven by curiosity. And like any good hip-hop DJ knows, it's curiosity that leads the way to unfamiliar beats and hidden hooks. For us, the thrill of diving into the unknown makes it all feel more fascinating, more interesting, more new.

BE INTRIGUED BY THE UNKNOWN!

Grow beyond your own current cultural experience! The unfamiliar is always unique, always different, always challenging, and always evokes creativity. Each time we look into the unfamiliar, we find opportunities to discover something that fuels our imagination - a new path leading to some place not yet explored. Because when you decide to explore the strange it never stays strange for long, but it becomes the beginning of a new journey.

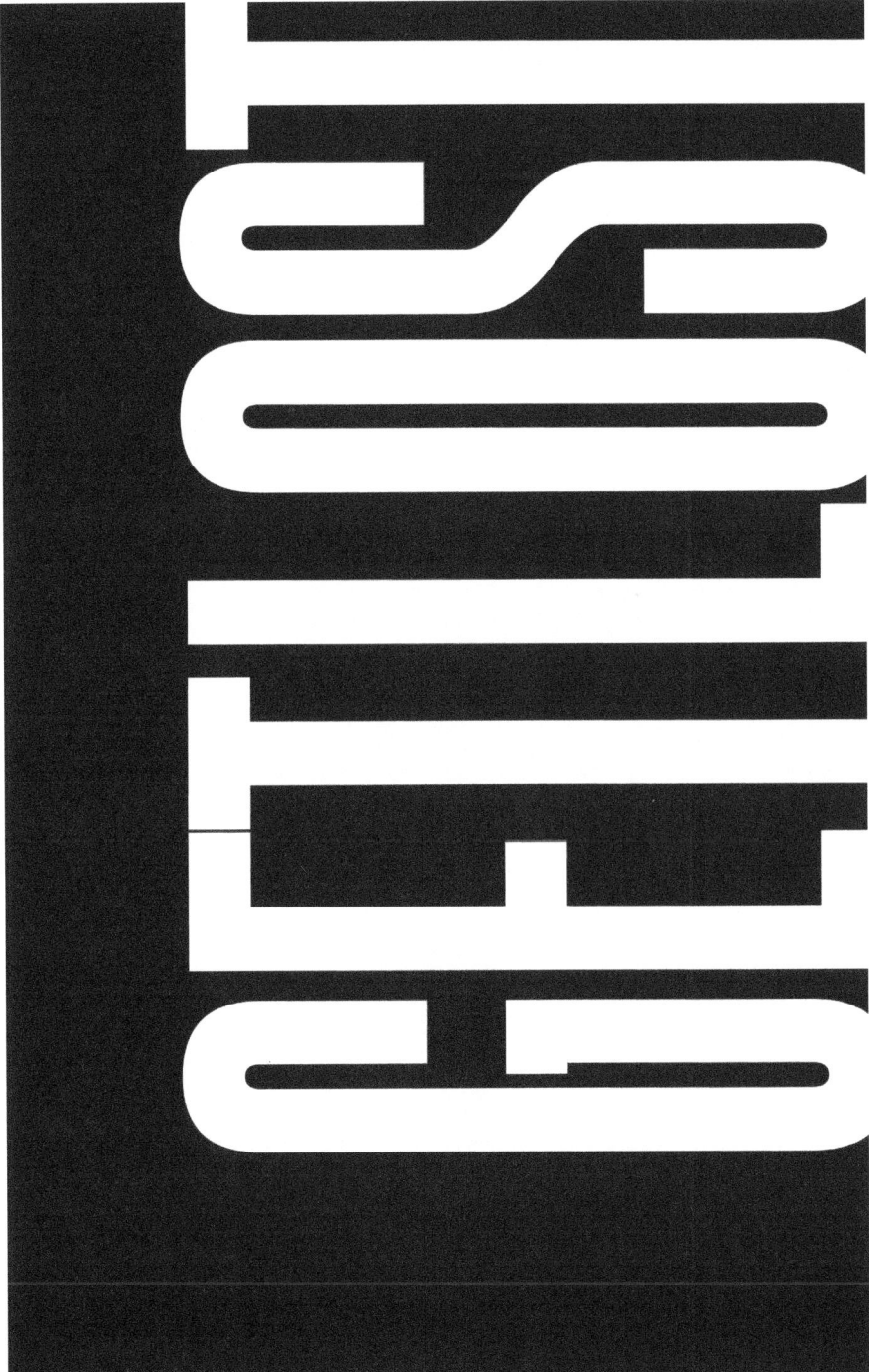

Imagine being lost in a 'strange' city where you have never been before and in order to find your way you start looking at everything more closely. Looking at what's familiar and what's unfamiliar. Paying attention to things you weren't even trying to look for. When you get lost you will use all of your senses (smelling, seeing, tasting, touching and hearing).

EXPLORE!

You'll start to notice things you usually don't notice, like the smell of food coming from an open window, the sound of words in a heated discussion, the way women wear their hats, the way men walk and express joy or anger, and how different languages resonate with you or which colors are considered to match. You are trying to make connections between what you have experienced in the past and what you are currently experiencing. And that's exactly how cultural DJing works. You make new connections and create clashes that result in noticing what you have not yet noticed.

THE FAMILIAR
+
THE UNFAMILIAR
=
THE UNEXPECTED

Surround yourself with smart and creative people of all ages and cultures. Look for creative connections in the worlds of art, design and music. If creators are frequently exposed to a variety of art and culture, they are naturally remixing the world. Just step into the kaleidoscope of life experiences that present you with a wild, magical base for your creative, borderless mix. In other words: immerse yourself into diverse authentic creative possibilities, become a cultural collector. However, this doesn't mean becoming a hoarder. Hoarders grab anything they find, but collectors select only things they are truly interested in.

Observing creative people from around the world presenting themselves in public gives you insights into how combining cultures to create an individual style has already become an important tool for multicultural communities. Being part of these ever-changing creative clusters leads to cultural exchanges and cultural remixes - including everything from how we dress to the music on our playlists, to what we eat and how we talk to our friends.

In a way, we are all working on becoming Cultural DJs already. But recognizing the creative bridges that are able to connect us and developing cultural empathy take practice. You practice, and each time you open up new pathways into the magical world of diversity. You are learning by doing and will soon discover that you are becoming more and more sensitive about how to mix, combine and fuse. You will develop more originality, imagination, and a stronger sense of empathy. Plus, you'll have lots of FUN!

THE
PO
WER
OF

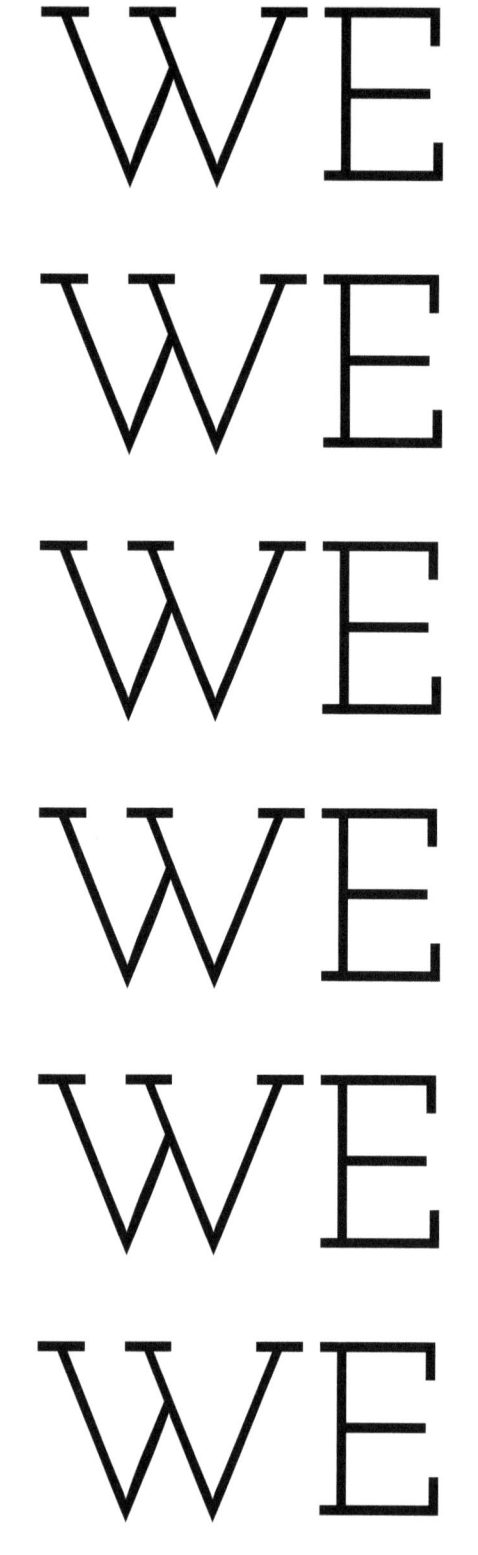

The power of WE lies in the connectivity of the creative process - and one of the major ingredients needed is being able to relate to your creative partners as equals. However, you will only be able to do this and fully embrace the unknown if your creative interaction is driven by cultural empathy.

A high level of trust is absolutely essential between the collaborating partners - which is different from collaborations that merely involve the sharing of labor. Cultural DJing requires the sharing of ideas, and just like during a brainstorming session, those ideas should not immediately be evaluated. The essential element of trust helps to be able to deal with initial ideas that might appear to be based on general assumptions or even stereotypes.

Cultural DJing promotes cultural empathy, which enables you to adopt a multiperspective way of seeing things by looking through the eyes of others. By practicing cultural empathy, you may even experience the sensation of seeing what has always been familiar to you, as something strange.

Our cultures provide us with an array of ways of thinking, speaking, hearing, and interpreting the world. Learning how to adopt foreign viewpoints, seeing things through the eyes of others, accepting diverse cultural perspectives, and trying to understand the origin of generalizations and stereotypes helps to bring down barriers and bridge the language and preperception gap.

A great way to achieve this is using the universal languages of creativity: All musicians speak music, all dancers understand movement and visual artists communicate through images.

HOT CAN
BE COOL,
COOL CAN
BE HOT,
EACH CAN
BE BOTH.
BUT HOT
OR COOL,

JAZZ IS JAZZ

— LOUIS ARMSTRONG

We strongly believe that one's culture is not based on passports but on personal experiences and values. To us culture means shared patterns and interactions of behavior in a particular group of people or society. Culture is not stale, but is subject to constant change. Many people still believe that culture, especially their own, should be prevented from changing and always stay the same. Yet throughout history all cultures of the world survived and expanded by adapting to, merging and fusing with other cultures. Those that didn't or couldn't, just died.

Adding different cultural point of views is similar to adding new instruments to an orchestra. Each new tone is a unique contribution and has a unique value. And no two tones or musicians will make the same contribution.

THE ART OF BEING UNIQUE ... TOGETHER.

WE all become the sum of who and what we choose to add to our lives. Note that our approach is not about cross-cultural communications aimed at selling a product or a service. At its best, a Cultural DJ will always showcase cultural authenticity and not cultural appropriation, which is based on stealing. We understand that every culture has its own strengths and weaknesses, but when cultural empathy drives the creative exchange there is a real chance to turn diverse cultural experiences into something new, something authentic and something courageous.

We've found from our own experiences working on many multicultural projects around the world that making connections and building trust can sometimes be difficult - especially when language is a barrier.

Some people may fear that if they open up to different cultures they might end up diluting their own. In fact, we are not promoting giving up your personal uniqueness at all. Actually, you should understand your own culture before you venture out to experiment. Keeping a strong point of view does not mean being inflexible. It just makes sure that your own essence is present to serve as a foundation for collaboration. Also, only when you have your own point of view, will you be able to understand, tolerate or even identify with and accept somebody else's.

Think of an artist trying to get the color purple by mixing blue and red. If she takes undiluted blue and adds undiluted red, the effect will be an intense, bright purple. But the more water she adds to the blue or red prior to mixing, the paler the result will be.

Working with interesting artists and creators from various cultures in multicultural creative clusters is always rewarded with originality, innovation and creative thinking.

Cultural DJs need to enable connections between people who may play any number of roles in the creative process while still contributing their own uniqueness. In any remix there are basic roles that need to be filled. Cultural DJs are not committees dealing only with the conception of a project. They must also produce and present to an audience.

NO
CULTURE
CAN LIVE
IF IT
ATTEMPTS
TO BE
EXCLUSIVE

- Mahatma Gandhi

A cultural remix is a creative collaboration between what came before and what is to come

- NormanSusanne

There are three main stages of a creative cultural collaboration. What makes creative cultural collaborations unique is that they not only promote different cultural experiences but add to them.

THE DESIGN STAGE

This first stage of a creative cultural collaboration should involve the fewest number of collaborators possible. Each additional person involved at this stage reduces the chance of the critical free flowing exchange of ideas. Ideally it should be made up of two individuals with different talents, unique ways of working and diverse backgrounds and experiences. They should have a similar level of creative passion and a mutual desire to collaborate. And of course both must be open to accept possibilities for solutions that may come from anywhere.

THE EXECUTION STAGE

The execution or production stage requires pushing the ideas forward that were developed in the first stage while interacting with the larger group of contributors. You can think of it as a team in a relay-race, passing ideas to each other the way runners pass a baton. Each team member has the responsibility to push the idea forward while adding his or her own unique talents to the race.

THE SHARING STAGE

Just like in hip hop culture, interaction with the audience is one of the most important ingredients in the concept of remixing the world. You get the audience to play its part in mixing the familiar with the unfamiliar. By comforting and startling the audience at the same time, your remixes will lead to reactions to the new.

A creative network of various team-players from diverse backgrounds is needed for the art of remixing the world.

THE CULTURAL DJs

Cultural DJs are at the center of a remix and are synchronized on an equal basis regarding the overall conception, production and sharing of the project. Each one involved ultimately takes full responsibility for what is done. This core team works best as a small group of mix masters who have established trust and respect for each other but also have contributed unique cultural experiences to the mix.

THE PARTNERS

Partners supply funds, resources and may even be part of the overall concept of the project, but must pass on the execution to the collaborators - just like a film producer chooses a director and then lets her create the film with her own team. Partners do not necessarily have to play a role in the creative collaboration itself, but they can greatly influence its relationship to the outside world.

THE CREATIVE TEAMS

All members of the creative teams should buy into the intentions and visions of the project set by the Cultural DJs and contribute their own unique expertise. Ideally, their contributions will exceed what the initial specs require.

THE SUPPORT TEAMS

Support teams are chosen because they can identify and solve specific issues needed and usually don't stray far from the specifications they receive. Unlike the creative teams, support teams should not surprise you. Their role is to be competent.

THE AUDIENCE

Making the audience or end user part of the creative collaboration by creating an emotional connection is the goal of every DJ. Consideration of the audience is one of the main factors involved in the successful outcome of a remix, and its perceived needs, desires and expectations should not be overlooked.

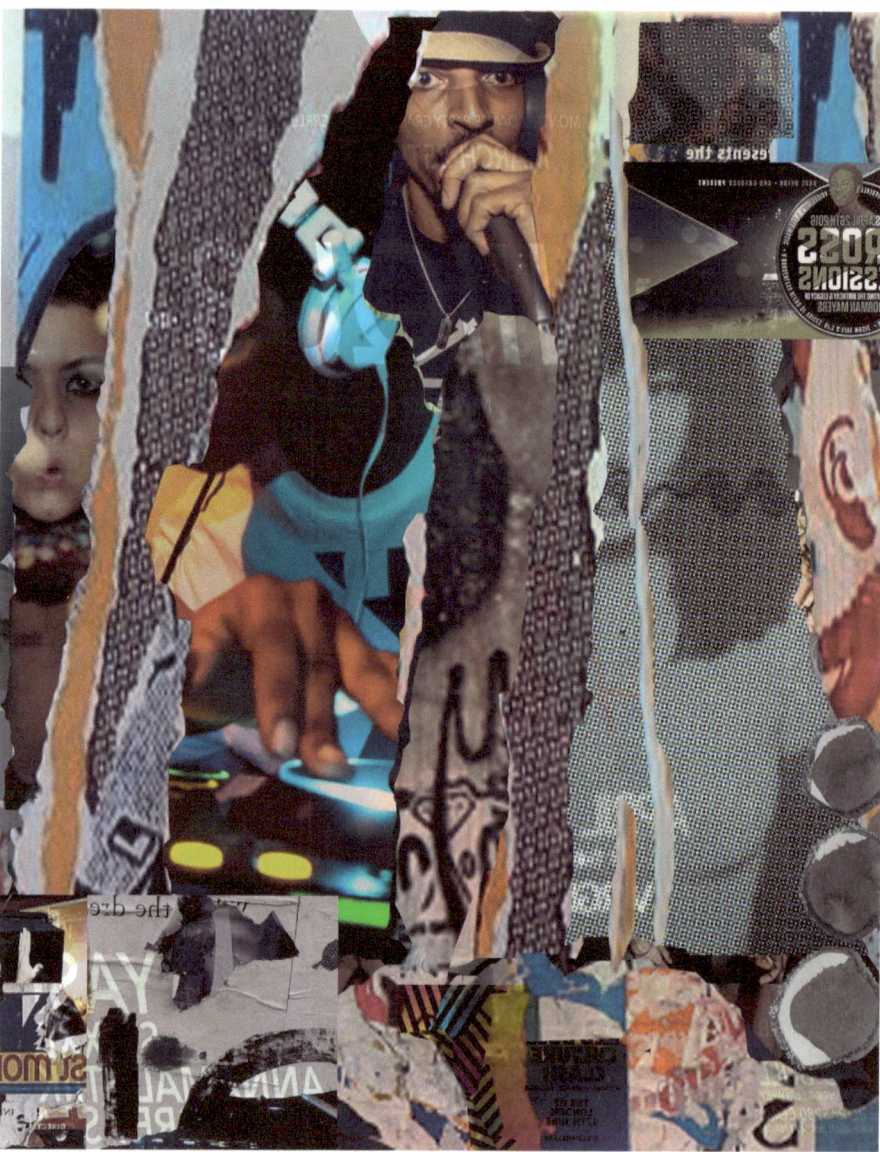

NU
NESS

is
the fusion
of the
unfamiliar
and the
familiar

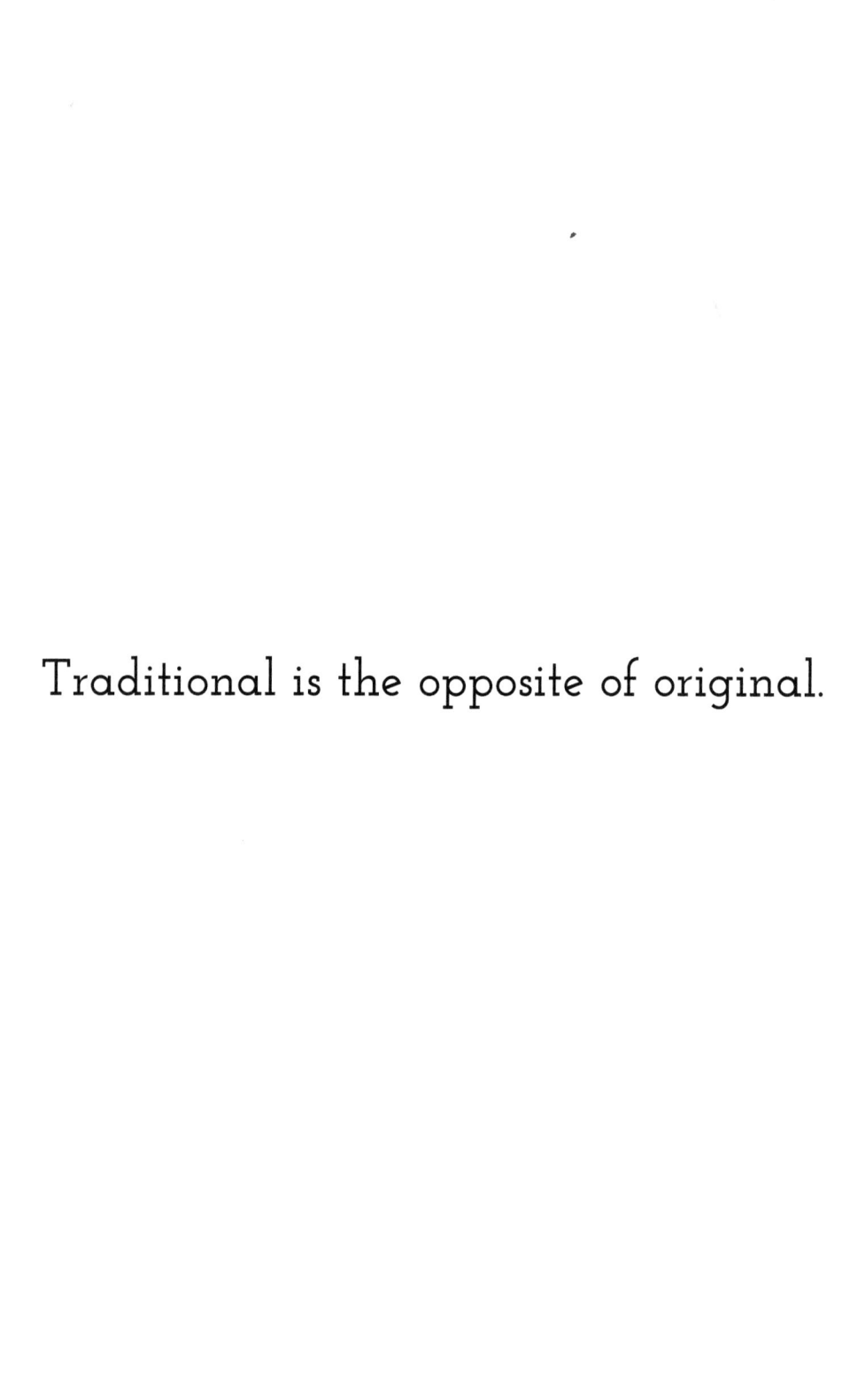

Traditional is the opposite of original.

Cultural DJs understand how to mix what we know with what we don't know yet. A simple yet powerful way to change perspectives when collaborating with creative people from different cultures is to just ask yourself...

WHAT IF?

WHAT IF? gives you the permission to think the opposite of what the audience expects, and it can be an extremely exciting way to unleash one's imagination. Start by combining elements that seem to not fit or appear to even be the opposites of each other. Try placing culturally familiar images into different cultural situations.

WHAT IF? we mixed Eastern European tribal face designs with pre-Columbian art? Or **WHAT IF?** we combined Nollywood storytelling with carnival in Rio? Or **WHAT IF?** we fused the music from our parents' record collection with the LA art scene?

Sample elements from different cultures, then examine if they have something in common, such as a similar function or a shared characteristic. Create a new definition or put a refreshing spin on tradition and ask yourself …
WHAT IF?

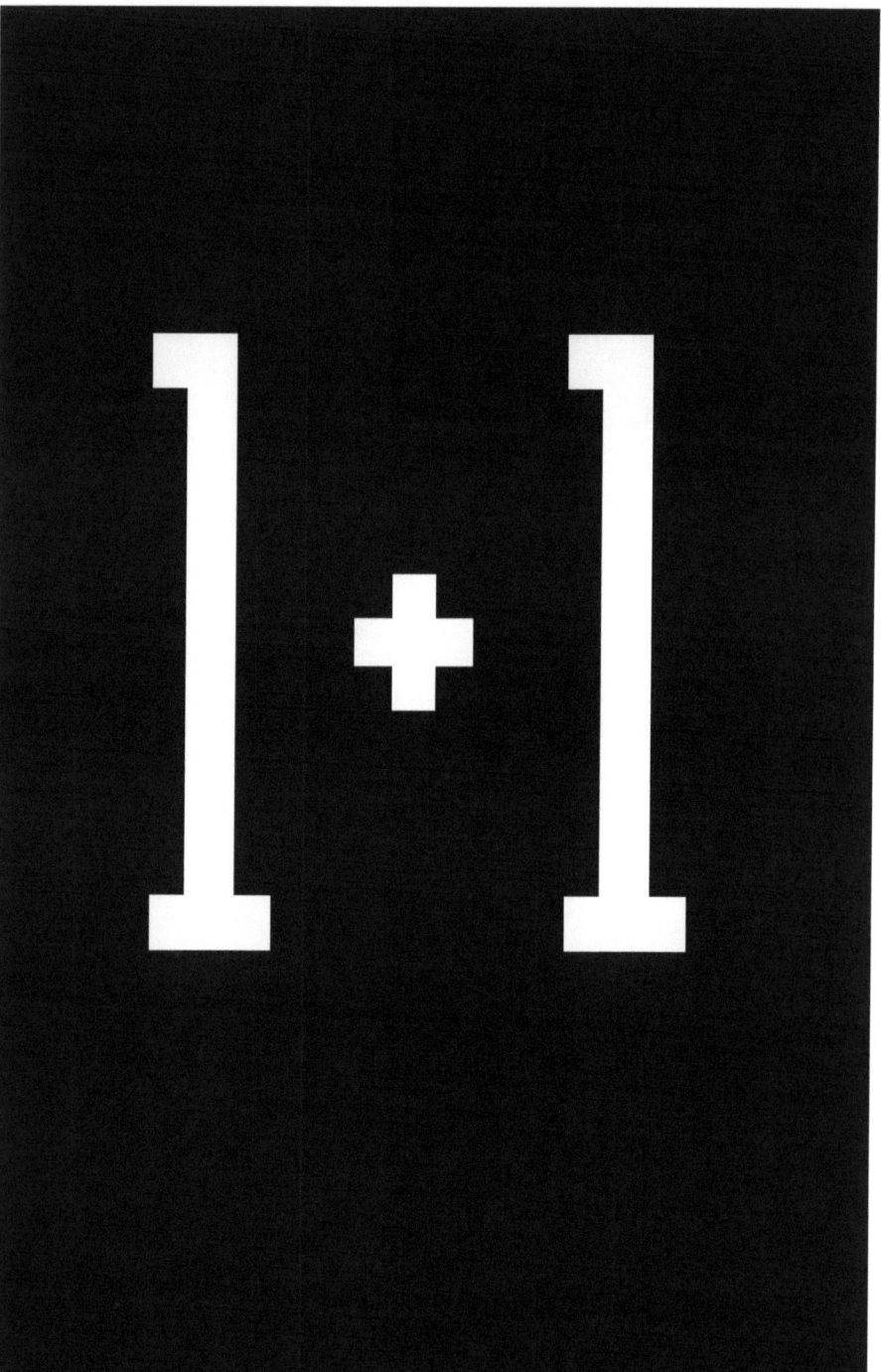

=3=1

This amazing formula 1 + 1 = 3 = 1 is what we call DJ math: When two unique elements become more than the sum of their original parts, and then are fused together to become one - and finally emerge as something completely new.

A good example for this approach is The West Indian PepperPot.

For this popular Caribbean meal, each day from the beginning of the week, different leftovers are added to a pot with a base of herbs and spices (which serve as preservatives). And by the end of the week all of the different fragments and ingredients of that week's various food additions are mixed, combined and fused together into a one-of-a-kind, delicious dish. By just remixing different meals, a totally new meal is created.

If we begin to look at the world this way, we will automatically stop looking at what's different about people as something to stay away from, but as an asset to embrace and an opportunity to remix. For creative people, cultural diversity can be a big delicious PepperPot. When we find something interesting to add to our pot, we can add it in a way that fuses different unique flavors, with each of the unique ingredients clearly tastable.

The uniqueness of cultural DJing lays in the exclusion of what is termed cultural appropriation - where people pick and steal single elements from cultural content and add them to their own, often even based on the idea of exploitation.

Cultural DJs, however, are able to fuse cultural ideas through the process of true collaboration.

The things that make us different, those are our superpowers.

- Lena Waithe

CREATIVECULTURALCOLLABORATIONS

REMIXTHEWORLD

YOU
can

remix
the world

by...

talking to strangers, hanging out with creative geniuses, bringing your own flava, not inventing anything but reinventing everything, being multi-local, letting the world inspire you, using the power of WE, saying "FUCK IT", making your mark, having an open mind, rejecting preconceived boundaries, just listening, making 1 + 1 = 3 and then 1 again, changing perspectives, being a cultural collector, exploring, thinking with your hands, developing nu-ness, letting your curiosity lead you, retelling stories, blowing up shit, following your passion, expanding your horizons, observing closely, never growing up, creating poems, changing your tools, playing, letting cultural diversity drive your creativity, creating global hybrids, re-framing the familiar, being a pioneer, fusing ideas, embracing the strange, being YOU, breaking rules, developing cultural empathy, cross-pollinating, traveling through time, bringing down barriers, creating communities, being culturally authentic, mastering a skill, flipping and flowing, really caring for something, being global, enhancing your cultural I.Q., stepping away from your screen, mixing what you know with what you don't know, starting a revolution, asking WHAT IF?

The best thing about Cultural DJs is that they are everywhere. Cultural DJs can be found in every city, in every country and in every culture. We can use the power to remix diverse cultural experiences and produce NU-NESS from anywhere in the world to just make things prettier, or to produce things that improve people's lives or the state of our planet - and decide to rock the world.

It doesn't
matter where
you are coming from
I smell creativity

- Brian Tracy Don Draper

THE MOVE MENT

THE NETWORK is a database that provides Cultural DJs with the possibility to find other creators, organizations, institutions, projects, initiatives, and services they need to realize their creative collaborative projects - worldwide.

You find the larger, constantly updated version of THE NETWORK on our website:
www.borderlesscreativity.org

CRECUCO - a global initiative that fosters the relationship between creativity, cultural diversity and collaboration. www.crecuco.co

FABRICA - a research centre that offers young people from around the world the opportunity for creative multicultural, multidisciplinary interchange. www.fabrica.it

THE CREATIVE ALLIANCE - the goal is to match up powerful initiatives with powerful creators. www.civicnation.org/creative

CAMEO KOLLEKTIV - provides open spaces for intercultural exchange with the aim to network people through creative projects. www.cameo-kollektiv.de

DESIGN INDABA - based on an annual festival in South Africa bringing together creative people from around the world. www.designindaba.com

CROSS CULTURAL COLLABORATIVE - a nonprofit educational organization that promotes cultural exchange encouraging participants to find rewards in different forms of art. www.culturalcollaborative.org

WINGS AND ROOTS - a transmedia, transnational community project that is re-imagining beyond traditional borders. www.withwingsandrootsfilm.com

SA CREATIVES - a platform where individuals can connect with fellow creatives, promote their work, share ideas and collaborate with like-minded individuals. www.sacreativenetwork.co.za

THNK - develops and supports creative leadership around the world with the purpose to resolve societal challenges. www.thnk.org

ART THERAPY WITHOUT BORDERS - promoting international art therapy initiatives in mental health, healthcare, and education worldwide. www.atwb.org

THE CREATORS PROJECT - VICE's arts and culture platform, covering every aspect of the creative process. They have collaborated with more than 600 artists globally. www.creators.vice.com

COLORS MAGAZINE - created by photographer Oliviero Toscani and art director Tibor Kalman in 1991 to show the world to the world. The message has remained the same: diversity is good. www.colorsmagazine.com

INSIDE OUT PROJECT - a global art project using photographic portraits to share the untold stories and images of people in their communities. www.insideoutproject.net

TRAVEL PHOTOGRAPHER SOCIETY - its mission is to promote the work and expertise of photographers from across the globe. www.travelphotographersociety.com

DESIGN EXCHANGE - a creative multidisciplinary global network devoted to the exchanging of ideas. www.demagazine.co.uk

CREATIVE EDUCATION FOUNDATION - (CEF) is a nonprofit organization that mobilizes leaders in the field of creative theory and practice. www.creativeeducationfoundation.org

CREATIVE ROOTS - an ever-growing blog representing nations through art and design. www.creativeroots.org

MAGNUM FOUNDATION - expands creativity and diversity in documentary photography. www.magnumfoundation.org/magnumfoundationfund

COMEDIA - develops projects concerned with city life, culture and creativity. www.comedia.org.uk

THE CREATIVE WORK FUND - invites artists and nonprofit organizations to create new artworks through collaborations. www.creativeworkfund.org

DR MONK - an international innovation agency, with headquarters in Amsterdam and Accra. www.drmonk.org

ARTE TV - stands for cultural diversity, encourages artistic creativity, and promotes Europe's cultural heritage. www.arte.tv

BOMBAY FLYING CLUB - an international storytelling agency deeply rooted in collaborative photojournalism. www.bombayfc.com

ONE BILLION RISING - the biggest mass action to end violence against women in human history. www.onebillionrising.org

BURN - brings together photographers from around the world to collaborate with the master photographer David Alan Harvey. www.burnmagazine.org

100 CAMERAS - gives kids from marginalized communities across the globe the tools to express themselves through photography. www.100cameras.org

SEEME - connects the world's creators to a global audience both online and in world-class, real-world exhibitions. www.see.me

CONTEÃ‚´ MAGAZINE - their mantra is all about collaboration and some of Africa's best creatives. www.contemag.com/contemag

THE CREATIVE FINDER - a global platform for creative content, collaboration and discovery. www.thecreativefinder.com

NOWNESS - a global movement for creative excellence in storytelling. www.nowness.com

THE CENTER FOR ARTISTIC ACTIVISM - a place to explore, analyze, and strengthen connections between social activism and artistic practice. www.artisticactivism.org

VAWAA - helps you discover and book vacations around the world with artists who are masters of their craft and creative ambassadors. www.vawaa.com

VSCO - an art and technology company empowering people everywhere to create, discover, and connect. www.vsco.co

ADCE's - their mission is to connect the European community to a borderless creative network. www.adceurope.org

CREATIVE CITIES NETWORK - currently formed by 116 members from 54 countries covering seven creative fields. www.en.unesco.org/creative-cities/home

DISTRICTS OF CREATIVITY - brings people together from across the globe and from various domains to promote and use the power of creative thinking. www.districtsofcreativity.org

CREATIVE VISIONS - inspires and empowers creative activism worldwide. www.creativevisions.org

CENTRE FOR CREATIVE ARTS - supports exchange opportunities and network development between African and international cultural practitioners. www.cca.ukzn.ac.za/index.php

SILKROAD - a collective fostering collaboration among artists and institutions, promoting multicultural artistic exchange. www.silkroadproject.org

MUSICIANS WITHOUT BORDERS - uses the power of music to bridge divides, connect communities, and heal the wounds of war. www.musicianswithoutborders.org

PLAYING FOR CHANGE - a movement created to inspire and connect the world through music. www.playingforchange.com

RED BULL ACADEMY - a world-traveling series of music workshops and festivals that gives creative participants from all over the world the chance to meet and collaborate. www.redbullmusicacademy.com

FETE DE LA MUSIQUE - an annual celebration of music in the streets of cities all over the world that takes place on June 21. www.fetedelamusique.culturecommunication.gouv.fr

THE NETWORK is currently managed by Norman Mayers and Susanne Heitz. We welcome all submissions that will add to our growing collection of international live and virtual organizations fusing creativity, cultural diversity and collaboration.

email us at: culturaldj@borderlesscreativity.org

IT'S ALL BEEN DONE BEFORE

BUT NOT THE WAY I DO IT

- Eva Tanguay

THANK YOU

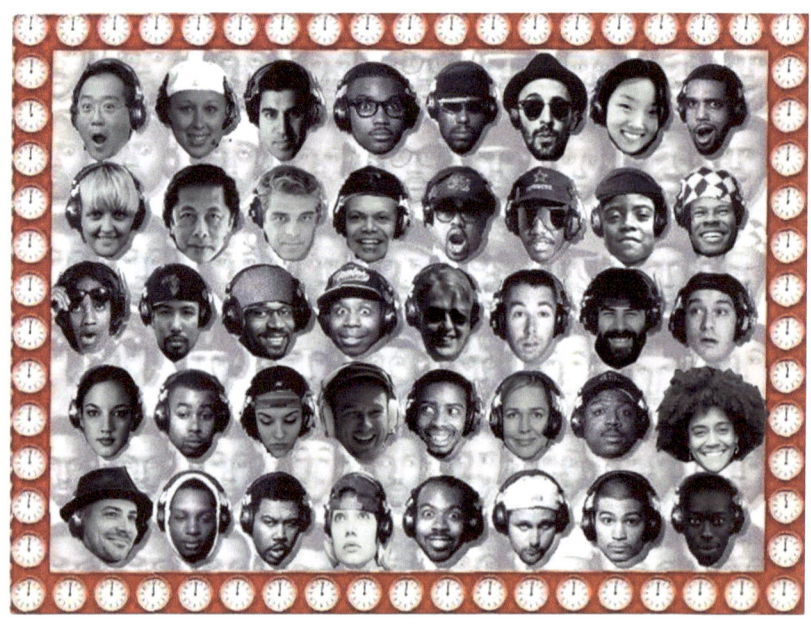

to all who helped make our book become a reality and to the many DJs we mixed, combined and fused with in order to complete this book, including, but not limited to: Annette Richter-Haschka, Ute Lindner, Achim Riemann, Nicola Turner, Ulrike Müller, John Jay, Kirby Ferguson, Tibor Kalman, Austin Kleon, Yo-Yo Ma, Selwyn Cambridge, Jenee Muyeau, James Rankin, Klaus Windolph, Sebastian Cunitz and Julius Matuschik.

Finally, we would like to thank all the Cultural DJs across the globe who continue to inspire us with their new and exciting creative cultural collaborations.

This book was created and produced by Norman Mayers + Susanne Heitz for red mango studios.
www.redmangostudios.com

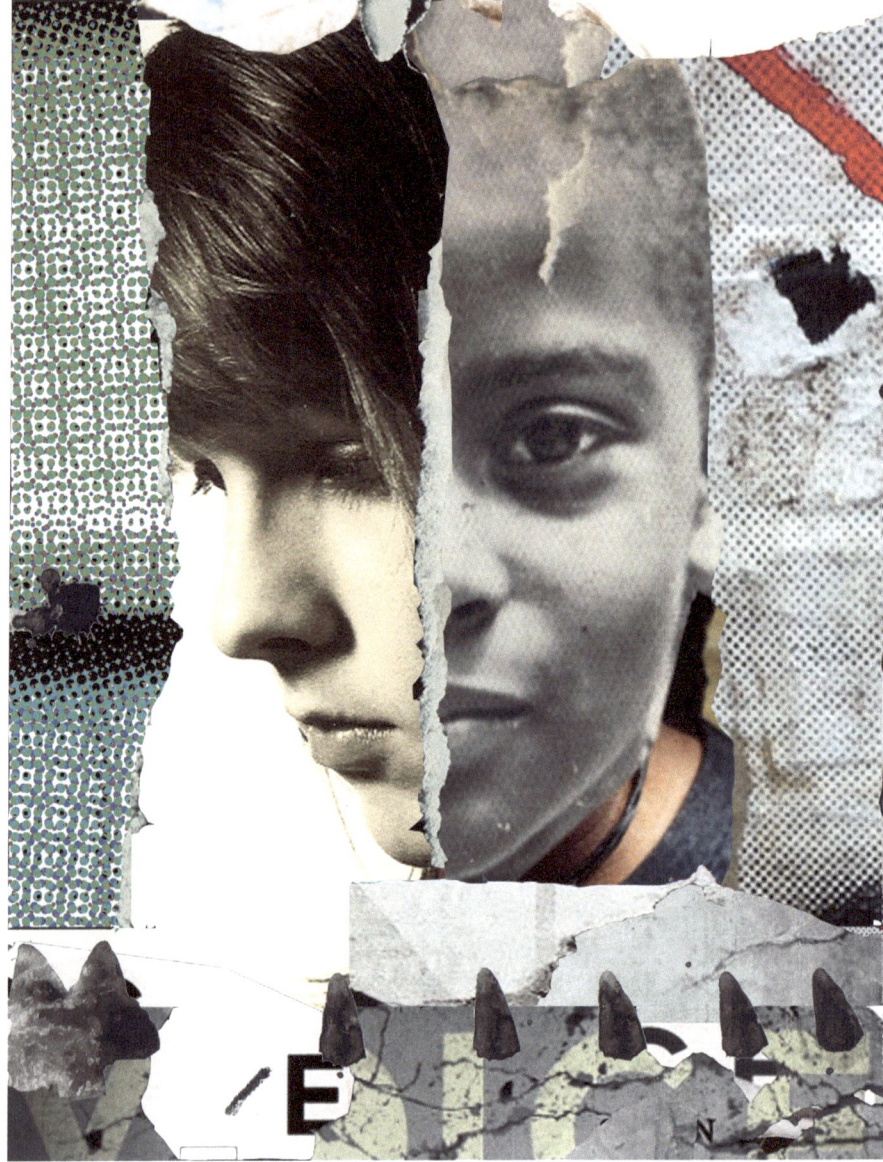

ABOUT THE AUTHORS

Norman Mayers is a lifelong ambassador to the borderless world of creativity. Since growing up in the Bronx during the early days of Hip-Hop, Norman has discovered countless ways to mix, combine and fuse his creativity with other Cultural DJs, visual explorers, musical storytellers and creative nomads from across the globe.

Born with an extra dose of imagination and the urge to create, Susanne Heitz' creative approach has always been driven by her passion to discover the unknown and to weave it into the tapestry of her work - be it as a visual artist with her work being collected around the world, as a writer for international clients, a designer and conductor of workshops or a collaborator with creative professionals.

Feel free to email us at redmango@hotmail.com.

We love to hear from you!

Cultural DJ

Second Edition: 2018

red mango studios

www.redmangostudios.com

Written by: Norman Mayers and Susanne Heitz

Art + Design by: NormSus

Copyright © 2018 CRECUCO LLC

You are free to share this work, with the understanding that you must give appropriate credit, provide a link to the license, and indicate if changes were made. You may do so in any reasonable manner, but not in any way that suggests the licensor endorses you or your use. You may not use the material for commercial purposes. If you remix, transform, or build upon the material, you must distribute your contributions under the same license as the original.

This is a human-readable summary of the Legal Code. The full license is available at:

https://creativecommons.org/licenses/by-nc-sa/3.0/

www.ingramcontent.com/pod-product-compliance
Lightning Source LLC
Chambersburg PA
CBHW040359220526
45473CB00025B/2530